Ten Little Llamas

W. Books

10 Ten Little Llamas
Jumping rope with a vine.

One became tangled so then there were . . .

One changed her mind
So then there were ...

One hurt his ankle so then there were . . .

6 Six Little Llamas
Out for a drive.

One decided to walk so then there were . . .

5 Five Little Llamas playing at the shore.

One forgot her pail so then there were . . .

One couldn't reach so then there were . . .

3 Three Little Llamas
On a hill with a view.

One left to find her dad so then there were . . .

2 Two Little Llamas
Out for a run.

One said he had run enough
So then there was ...

Hoping all her friends would remember to come over.

Hey, Isabelle here we all are,

And we didn't really have to come very far.